Here's
Another Book,
My Friend

HERE'S
ANOTHER BOOK,
MY FRIEND

* * *

Edited by
Robert Allan

STANYAN BOOKS   RANDOM HOUSE

A Stanyan book
Published by Stanyan Books,
8721 Sunset Blvd., Suite C
Hollywood, California 90069
and by Random House, Inc.
201 East 50th Street,
New York, N.Y. 10022

ISBN: 394-47376-0

Library of Congress Catalogue
Card Number: 75-170312

Printed in U.S.A.

Designed by Hy Fujita

For
EILEEN & CAROL O'BRIEN

A friend is a present
which you give yourself.
                    - ROBERT L. STEVENSON

My friends are my estate.
Forgive me then the
avarice to hoard them!
— EMILY DICKINSON

Go often to the house of
your friend, for weeds
choke up the unused path.
— CONFUCIUS

You can't fake friendship.
— BEVINS JAY

Our affections are our
life. We live by them;
they supply our warmth.
— WILLIAM CHANNING

Friendship is a word,
the very sight of which
in print makes the
heart warm.
— AUGUSTINE BIRRELL

Friendship consists in
forgetting what one
gives, and remembering
what one receives.
— ALEXANDRE DUMAS

Friendship is almost
always the union of
a part of one mind with
a part of another;
people are friends in
spots.
— SANTAYANA

There is nothing so great
that I fear to do for my
friend, nor nothing so
small that I will disdain
to do for him.
 — SIR PHILIP SIDNEY

Friendship is Love,with-
out either flowers or
veil.
 — J.C. AND A.W.HARE

It is best to live as
friends with those in
time with whom we would
be to all eternity.
 — THOMAS FULLER

Ah friendship, stronger
in thy might than time
and space!
 — HELEN HUNT JACKSON

"He is my friend," I said.
"Be patient!" Overhead
the skies were drear and
dim;
and lo! the thought of
him smiled on my heart
and then the sun shone
out again!

> \- JAMES W. RILEY

Thou may be sure that he
who will tell thee of
thy faults is thy friend,
for he ventures thy dis-
like and doth hazard thy
hatred.

> \- SIR WALTER RALEIGH

There should be fences
even between friends.
But they should have
great holes in them.
                    - HABIB SAHABIB

One friend in a life-
time is much; two are
many; three are hardly
possible.
                    - HENRY ADAMS

If you're my friend,
you'll take no notice
of my shortcomings.
                    - HAZEL MASSY

Oblige with all your
soul that friend who
has made a present of
his own.

— SOCRATES

There are two sorts of
pity; one a balm and
the other a poison. The
first is realized by our
friends, the last by our
enemies.

— CHARLES SUMNER

Nothing gives such a
blow to friendship as
detecting another in
an untruth.

— HENRY HAZLITT

Our friendship will en-
dure as long as you wish
it to.

— BARBARA ARMAND

Two persons cannot long
be friends if they can-
not forgive each other's
little failings.
- JEAN de la BRUYERE

There can never be true
friendship without self-
respect, and unless soul
meets soul free from
self-seeking.
- HUGH BLACK

No man is useless while
he has a friend.
- ROBERT L. STEVENSON

It is a good thing to be
rich, and to be strong,
but it is a better thing
to be beloved of many
friends.
- EURIPIDES

Friendship's an abstract
of this noble flame,
'Tis love refined, and
purged from all its dross
The next to angels' love,
if not the same.

— KATHERINE PHILIPS

My enemies are now so
numerous, I'm thankful
for the friends I've
got -- however few.

— ALEXANDER DREY

The needle's eye is
wide enough for two
friends.

— JOHN ROEBUCK

In making dinner for a
friend, don't forget
the love.
                    - JEANNE MOREAU

Neither a borrower, nor
a lender be; for loan
oft loses both itself
and friend.
          - WILLIAM SHAKESPEARE

Better are the blows of
a friend than the false
kisses of an enemy.
                - THOMAS a BECKET

We can never replace a
friend; they are all
different.
                - J.C.von SCHILLER

FRIENDSHIP

JUST THE PERFECT
BLENDSHIP.
WHEN OTHER
FRIENDSHIPS HAVE
BEEN FORGOT,
OURS WILL STILL
BE HOT.

— Cole Porter

We were good friends.
By that I mean we were
good to each other.

        - KATHARINE HEPBURN

A friend may be found
and lost, but an old
friend can never be
found, and nature has
provided he cannot be
easily be lost.

        - SAMUEL JOHNSON

Friendship has no name
but love.

        - HABIB SAHABIB

We are all travelers in
the wilderness of this
world, and the best
that we find in our
travels is an honest
friend.

        - ROBERT L. STEVENSON

A friend is a fixer of
wheels.

> \- WALT DISNEY

Friendship often ends
in love; but love in
friendship - never.

> \- CHARLES COLTON

Instead of loving your
enemies, treat your
friends a little better.

> \- EDGAR W. HOWE

A friend is never chosen.
A secret sympathy, the
attraction of a thousand
nameless qualities, a
charm in the expression
of the countenance, even
in voice or manner, a
similarity of circum-
stances -- these are
the things that begin
attachment.

> \- ANNA BARBAULD

There must be something
in friendship to dis-
tinguish it from a com-
panion, a schoolfellow,
or a sweetheart. Friend-
ship may look in at any
one of these doors, but
it stays not anywhere
till it comes to be the
best thing in the world.
- JEREMY TAYLOR

A friend is somebody
who knows all about you,
but likes you anyway.
- ORSON WELLES

If we would build on a
sure foundation in
friendship, we must
love our friends for
their sakes rather than
for our own.
- CHARLOTTE BRONTË

My friend, it's just a
little game of poker.
A game of chance. Would
I cheat a friend?
                    - W.C.FIELDS

If you have something
nice to say to someone,
tell it now. They can't
hear you at their
funeral.
                    - BEVINS JAY

The friend given you by
circumstances over which
you have no control, was
God's own gift.
            - FREDERICK ROBERTSON

When friends ask, there
is no tomorrow... only
now.
                - ALEXANDER DREY

Friendship is the
holiest out-going of
the human heart.

> — H. CLAY TRUMBULL

Friendship renders
prosperity more bril-
liant, while it lightens
adversity by sharing it.

> — CICERO

Other people pity; a
friend helps.

> — JOSEPH NEWTON

Friday is everybody's
friend.

> — CORRINE LeMAYE

What sweetness is left
in life if you take away
friendship? It is like
robbing the world of
the sun.

— CICERO

Greater love hath no
man than this, that a
man lay down his life
for his friends.

— JOHN 15:13

If you would have
friends, be one.

— ELBERT HUBBARD

Actions, not words, are
the true criteria of
the attachment of
friends.

— GEORGE WASHINGTON

Just say we're good
friends.

— BARBRA STREISAND

Everyone's friend is no
one's.

— SCHOPENHAUER

To find a friend one
must close one eye --
to keep him, two.

— NORMAN DOUGLAS

You're my friend, so I
brought you this book.
I give you this flower.
I hand you my hand.

— JOHN MARVIN

In the hour of misery,
the eye turns to
friendship. In the hour
of gladness, what is our
want? It is friendship.

— WALTER S. LANDOR

Friends and Lovers
                    - BOOK TITLE

Friendly Persuasion
                    - FILM TITLE

Forgotten Friends
                    - SONG TITLE

Friends of Mr. Sweeney
                    - FILM TITLE

Friends, unlike fash-
ions, should never change.
                    - OLD SAYING

Friend Of The Family
                    - PLAY

Friendly Enemies
                    - FILM TITLE

Beautiful Friendship
        - SONG TITLE

Five thousand of my
closest personal
friends.
        - PARTY INVITATION BY
                MICHAEL TODD

A friend of the court
        - LEGAL TERM

My Little Friend
        - RECORD ALBUM

Special Friendships
        - BOOK TITLE

Friends of Bertha
        - LODGE EXPRESSION

Choose your friends
wisely.
        - SAYING

I am not so conceited
as to believe I have
any friends.

        - COCO CHANEL

We speak of "choosing,"
of "making" friends.
What we can "choose"
and "make" is not the
friend, but opportunity
for contact. When the
contact happens, some-
thing higher than our
will chooses for us.

        - WILLIAM GANNETT

There is something in
these trifles that
friends bestow upon
each other which is an
indication of their af-
fection. I believe
that one who preserves
a lock of hair, a sim-
ple flower, or any tri-
fle of my bestowing,
loved me.

        - WASHINGTON IRVING

I thank God far more
for friends than for my
daily bread -- for
friendship is the bread
of the heart.

> — MARY MITFORD

Behold, how good and
how pleasant it is for
brethren to dwell to-
gether in unity!

> — PSALMS 133:1

Friends are like melons.
Shall I tell you why?
To find one good, you
must a hundred try.

> — CLAUDE MERMET

There is no folly
equal to that of throw-
ing away friendship in
a world where friend-
ship is so rare.
> — EDWARD BULWER-LYTTON

The friendship between
two men is something
only a woman can destroy.
> — ERNEST HEMINGWAY

Let flattery be far re-
moved from friendship.
> — CICERO

Stick to a friend a
little in the wrong.
> — JOHN RANDOLPH

A friend must not be
injured, even in jest.

> — SYRUS

A day for toil, an
hour for sport,
But for a friend is
life too short.

> — RALPH W. EMERSON

Heaven gives us friends
to bless the present
scene.

> — EDWARD YOUNG

Friendship takes place
between those who have
an affinity for each
other, and is a natural
result. No professions
nor advances will avail.
> — HENRY DAVID THOREAU

He has no future who is
without friends to share
with him, and is
wasting his existence.
> — A. BRONSON ALCOTT

When we lose a friend
we die a little.
> — DR. LOUISA DUFFE
> BOOTH

Friendship should be
dealt with tenderly;
it is a sensible plant,
not a roadside thistle.
We must not expect our
friends to be above hu-
manity.
> — OUIDA

He was a good husband
-- he treated me more
like a friend than a
wife.

> — MADAME CURIE

Friendship needs to be
rooted in respect; but
love can live upon it-
self alone.

> — OUIDA

I want your words and
your voice, with your
thoughts, your looks,
and your gestures, to
interpret your feel-
ings.

> — HENRY VAN DYKE

A friend is one who in-
cessantly pays us the
compliment of expecting
from us all the virtues.

> — HENRY DAVID THOREAU

A friend is somebody
who loves us with un-
derstanding, as well
as emotion.
> — ROBERT L. STEVENSON

There is no friend like
an old friend who has
shared our morning
days, no greeting like
his welcome, no homage
like his praise.
> — OLIVER W. HOLMES

The soul needs friend-
ship, the heart needs
love.
> — ED HABIB

The making of friends
who are real friends is
the best token we have
of a man's success in
life.
> — EDWARD EVERETT HALE

Love is only chatter.
Friends are all that
matter.

— GELETT BURGESS

You, sir, are a foul-
weather friend.

- BERNARD BARUCH

I want someone to laugh
with me, someone to be
grave with me, and at
times, someone to admire
my acuteness.

- ROBERT BURNS

God make me worthy of
my friends.

- FRANK SHERMAN

It was a wound -- not
small. I helped him
up, knowing that he'd
not recover, I held
him like I would a
friend.

> — ROD McKUEN

Some of the finest
friendships are between
persons of different
dispositions. The mind
is often attracted by
perfections it lacks it-
self.

> — EUSTACE BUDGELL

Friends are the thermo-
meters by which we may
judge the temperature
of our fortunes.

> — LADY BLESSINGTON

HAIL!

HAIL!

THE GANG'S

ALL HERE.

WHAT THE HELL

DO WE CARE!

                    - D.A.Estrom

Every man needs a
friend. I have many and
I wouldn't trade them
for all the world offers.

> — LYNDON B. JOHNSON

A "common friendship"
-- who talks of a com-
mon friendship? On
earth no word is more
sublime.

> — HENRY DRUMMOND

My friend peers in on
me with merry
Wise face, and though
the sky stays dim,
The very light of day,
the very
Sun's self comes in
with him.

> — ALGERNON SWINBURNE

Friendship is the great-
est luxury of life.

> — EDWARD EVERETT HALE

Who's your friend?
                    - MAE WEST

Friendship doubles our
joy and divides our
grief.
                    - CICERO

How good it feels,the
hand of an old friend!
                    - HENRY LONGFELLOW

I awoke this morning
with devout thanks-
giving for my friends.
                    - RALPH W. EMERSON

In prosperity our
friends know us; in ad-
versity we know our
friends.
                    - JOHN C. COLLINS

Oh my friend, you have
no way of knowing how
longingly I look at you.

       — WALT WHITMAN

The comfort of having a
friend may be taken
away, but not that of
having had one.

> — SENECA

Feed a friendship apples,
caress it with soft
smiles.

> — ALEXANDER DREY

No distance of place or
lapse or time can lessen
the friendship of those
who are thoroughly per-
suaded of each other's
worth.

> — ROBERT SOUTHEY

There are no rules for
friendship. It must
be left to itself. We
cannot force it any
more than love.

> — WILLIAM HAZLITT

A friend is dearer than
the light of heaven.
        - ST. JOHN CHRYSOSTOM

How were friendship po-
sible? In mutual devo-
tedness. Ten men, uni-
ted in love, are capa-
ble of doing what ten
thousand singly would
fail in. Infinite is
the help man can yeld
to man.
        - THOMAS CARLYLE

Perhaps the most de-
lightful friendships
are those in which
there is much agree-
ment, much disputa-
tion, and yet more
personal liking.
        - GEORGE ELIOT

A friend is what the
heart needs all the time.
        - HENRY VAN DYKE

When we are young,
friends are taken for
granted. When we are
old, we know what it
means to have them.

> — EDVARD GRIEG

Friendships always be-
nefit, while love some-
times injures.

> — SENECA

Madam, I have been look-
ing for a person who
disliked gravy all my
life; let us swear
eternal friendship.

> — SYDNEY SMITH

To desire the same
things and to reject
the same things, consti-
tutes true friendship.

> — SALLUST

SHOULD

AULD

ACQUAINTANCE

BE FORGOT

AND NEVER

BROUGHT TO

MIND...

        - Robert Burns

Don't fiddle with your
friends - be true.
> — BEVINS JAY

You can lay the foun-
dation of a friendship
in a matter of moments,
but it is a work of time
to build the monument
> — MADELYN WATT

Friends -- those rela-
tions one makes for
one's self.
> — EUSTACHE DESCHAMPS

Chance makes brothers
-- hearts make friends.
> — DR. DUANE BOOTH

We're after the same
rainbow's end, waitin'
round the bend, my
huckleberry friend...

— JOHNNY MERCER
& HENRY MANCINI

The things our friends
do with us and for us
form a portion of our
lives; they strengthen
our personality.

> — GOETHE

Form friendships, not
attachments.

> — WAYNE MASSIE

Friends are the end and
the reward of life.
They keep us worthy of
ourselves; and when we
are alone, we are only
nearer to the absent.

> — ROBERT L. STEVENSON

The supreme happiness
of life is the convic-
tion of being loved for
yourself, or, more cor-
rectly, being loved in
spite of yourself.

> — VICTOR HUGO

Friendship is an un-
selfish affection for
another because he is
better than we -- or
ought to be, as we see
it.

> \- H.CLAY TRUMBULL

Pity and friendship are
passions incompatible
with each other.
Friendship is made up
of esteem and pleasure;
pity is composed of
sorrow and contempt.

> \- OLIVER GOLDSMITH

Don't foul our friend-
ship with cheap love.

> \- MAE THOMSON DWYER

Fixin' up friendships,
that's my job.

> \- FATHER GRACE

A friend in need is a
friend indeed.

                - WILLIAM HAZLITT